Abundance Struggles?

Don Barnes

Published by Don Barnes, 2024.

 **LifeWorksInThrees.com**

Table of Contents

About the Author

Don is the founder and author of Life Works in Threes!™ E-books. He is a lifelong Texan who has traveled extensively while taking a keen interest in human behavior. His curiosity about life and what drives humans led him to the discovery of how life works in threes. He coined this term as the *Tryune Concept.*

Don attended college on an athletic scholarship and then embarked on a 30-year career in the oil and gas industry. Since the year 2000, he has been a consultant for distributors and manufacturers of various industries. Along the way, he worked on his Tryune discovery in hopes of someday sharing his findings with those struggling unnecessarily... in life. What Don surmised from 40+ years of R&D was that people were struggling unnecessarily because they were not aware that "life works in threes." They, for the most part, have been living their lives <u>by chance</u> rather than <u>by choice,</u> he also discovered.

From this, he began focusing on the "mechanics of life" which shows formulas for success with subjects such as *life, health, money, purpose and so forth.* When people are able to grasp the Tryune Concept, they can apply the formulas with topics that interest them and begin eliminating the struggle. This epiphany is what triggered his Tryune venture and is now on the path of sharing with all who desire to improve on their lives.

Don currently resides in Southern California and Texas while overseeing his businesses and investments.

Life Works in Threes™

When I was a kid growing up, no one sat me down and said, "Okay Don, I'm going to show you how life works so that you can navigate your way through adulthood." I graduated from school, got married and went about my way with the "learn as you go" concept. It was kind of like putting together a backyard swing set without a set of instructions. Lots of frustration and do-overs, for sure!

My discovery of the "triune" word and noticing how things come together in threes is really what set me off on researching that maybe "life comes in three" ...sort of a mechanical approach to managing life, if you will. I combed the libraries and bookstores for information on this and found one book on the subject that was written back in 1951. The author's name was John S. Arant.

What Mr. Arant had to say is this "For lack of a better name, I have called this *The Triangle of Triumph* and therefore, consistent with the name, since most of these conclusions are built on the geometric figure of the triangle." He continued "All Life and all lives are seated in, and circumscribed by, the triangle. The Author and Source and Director of all life is Himself triune in character – Father, Son, and Holy Spirit. Man is of triple nature – body, mind, and spirit – and within those three there are many triangles – desires, development, decay; intellect, will, sensibilities. Of this "paced interlude in the midst of eternity" which we call time there is the triangle of Past, Present, and Future. Space – that limitless and measureless element of the physical universe – is best known in terms of Height, Breadth, and Depth. Try building yourself some triangles along the lines of your Will, your Work, your Way – You will find some interesting angles.

So, for the first time, I realized that life is designed in a mechanical way to come in threes. That means you don't have to rely on wishing and hoping things turn out okay. You can actually look at the three parts that a particular thing is made of and then apply them to get what you're wanting. Like a three-ingredient recipe or a combination lock. With a combination lock, you need the three exact numbers to unlock the lock...otherwise you will continue to struggle.

Some 40 years later, I accumulated things that work in threes and that's when I knew I needed to share this with anyone wanting answers. To have success/harmony in your life, just apply the three parts of an area you're working on, and things will fall into place. I also learned that the recipe for success with just about anything is by doing these three things, consistently – THINK positively, SPEAK positively and ACT positively. For example, if I want to be a successful artist. I would think to myself "I can do this because I have the talent." Then I would speak it this way "Yes, I am working on my art degree and plan to do portraits professionally." Finally, I would act on that by taking art classes and continue crafting my skill. Eventually, I will see the positive results/success I'm looking for.

Conversely, if I think positively but speak negatively...it will cancel out. Or if I speak positively but have no positive action going on...nothing will happen.

I looked up "How Life Works" and "The Mechanics of Life" and these are really talking about the biology of how our cells work and other chemistry. TRYUNE WORKS! teaches that life is kind of like building blocks. Pick a topic you may be struggling with. See the three parts that topic consists of and then start applying them...on a consistent basis. That will help you overcome the struggle and get you back in harmony/success with how life works.

For 30+ years I was a golf instructor (by accident). My two kids had some success playing junior golf and so friends and neighbors would ask me to show them and their kids how to play golf successfully. From all of this, I got pretty good at watching golfers on the driving range and could spot right away why they were struggling with hitting bad golf shots. I was able to do that because I knew the three steps to hitting good golf shots. I learned them from studying golf and played for several decades. I "broke the code" for me so to speak.

So now you know that life works in threes. You can live your life *by choice* rather than *by chance* and that my friend... is the key to a fulfilling life.

LIFE WORKS IN THREES!

My sanctuary on the Pacific coast

Introduction

Abundance in a person's life goes beyond just material wealth—it's about experiencing a profound sense of fullness and richness in various aspects of life. Imagine waking up each day with a heart full of gratitude, surrounded by loving relationships that uplift you and bring joy to your soul. It's about having the freedom to pursue your passions and dreams, knowing that you have the resources and support to make them a reality.

In practical terms, abundance might mean having a fulfilling career that aligns with your values and talents, where you feel challenged and rewarded. It could also mean enjoying good health that allows you to fully engage in life's adventures and activities. Abundance often manifests as a deep sense of inner peace and contentment, where you trust in the flow of life and believe in your own resilience to overcome challenges.

Moreover, abundance can be found in the richness of experiences and memories created with friends and family—moments that money can't buy but which enrich your life beyond measure. It's about finding beauty in everyday moments, whether it's savoring a delicious meal, marveling at the wonders of nature, or simply sharing laughter with loved ones. Ultimately, abundance is a mindset—a way of seeing and appreciating the countless blessings that surround us, fostering a sense of fulfillment and happiness that extends far beyond material possessions.

My discovery of the Tryune Concept

Before we dive into adundance struggles and how to overcome them, let me share my discovery of the Tryune Concept and how life works in threes. It all began in the summer of 1982.

I grew up with parents who treated everyone with decency and respect. My three older sisters and I were raised in a home that was "middle-class traditional." We lived in modest homes in different small towns, attended school and church on a regular basis and celebrated all the traditional holidays. Eventually we settled during the spring of 1964 in the big city of Houston, Texas. I'll never forget the vastness of the city and hearing sirens from police cars, fire trucks and ambulances on a regular basis. I was excited and scared at the same time.

Once settled in this fast-paced city, I finished my growing-up years with an academic diploma and sweetheart intact. I got a job, bought a car, got married, bought a house and produced two beautiful babies in a span of about 5 years. Talk about having to grow up fast!

Things went from great in my childhood to absolute misery in my young adulthood. I began to struggle with my job because deep down I just hated what I was doing. This problem created a snowball effect because soon after, my weight, my finances, my relationships, my happiness and everything else worth saving was going down the drain. I eventually hit a level of frustration that I had never experienced before and didn't know how to get out of it. My cry for help was for anyone or anything to come to my rescue. I just ran out of solutions for my situation.

This is when my discovery happened.

One night shortly after my meltdown, while sleeping soundly, the word "triune" began to softly pound in my head like a mantra. I woke up a little startled and decided to go look up the word in my favorite dictionary (this was WAY before Google.) The definition said '**triune** (try-une) – 1) a group of three things; united. 2) Being 3 in 1 such as *humans are mental, physical and spiritual.* I scratched my head, got a glass of water and went back to bed.

The next day while driving around town, I began thinking about things that I was taught in my younger years that came in threes. My Boy Scout manual taught that to have **character**, I needed to be *1) physically strong,* 2) *mentally awake and 3) morally straight.* My high school football coach would say emphatically "If you want to be **a good football player**, you have to be *1) mobile 2) agile and 3) hostile!*" My first sales manager shared with me that to be **a successful salesman**, I needed to have *1) sales skills, 2) product knowledge and 3) a good image.*

"Hmm", I thought, "wonder if there are other examples out there of things that work in threes?" So, some 40 years later, I have researched and discovered that many, many things work in threes. What this message was telling me is that to achieve success or balance in any significant area of my life, the three things that area consisted of had to be present continuously. That's when I had my epiphany. This discovery was telling me the secret to how life <u>really</u> works.

Tryune is a play on the word "triune" as an invitation to "try" this concept. Furthermore, we do not say that life <u>only</u> works in threes. Life also works in ones, twos, fours and so on. What has been observed though is that the many things significant to life, just so happen to come and work in threes. That's what is being shared in this book.

Now, you are about to see 40+ years of research and proof that life works in threes. I did not make up any of these topics. I invite you to research them on the internet to validate what is written here. There are some interesting facts that most of us have never realized...until now.

How Life Works in Threes (around 200 examples)

<u>LIFE</u>

Humans consist of *body, mind and soul.*

A human's basic needs are *health, income and provisions.*

A human's basic wants are *comfort, gain and approval.*

Our minds are made up of the *conscious, the subconscious and the unconscious.*

Philosophy explains *the id, the ego and superego.*

Atoms consist of *protons, neutrons and electrons.*

Motion is explained by *three basic laws.*

Science falls under three main branches: *natural, social and formal sciences*

Time is *past, present and future*...at the same time.

Electricity consists of *ohms, amperes and voltage.*

Music's basic elements are *duration, pitch and timbre.*

Democracy is a government *of the people, by the people and for the people.*

U.S. branches of government are *the judicial, the executive and the legislative.*

Armed Forces protect us on *land, air and sea.*

Environmentally, we are asked *to reduce, recycle and re-use.*

The news program gives us *the news, sports and conditions.*

Our days consist of *morning, afternoon and evening.*

Three months in each season of the year

Our main meals are known as *breakfast, lunch and dinner.*

A balanced diet consists of *good proteins, carbohydrates and fats.*

Traditional Family consists of *father, mother, and child(ren)*

<u>SCIENCES</u>

Three major branches of natural science – *(physical, earth/space and life sciences)*

Three major branches of modern physics - *(classical, relativistic, quantum)*

Three major branches of biology *(botany, zoology, microbiology)*

Three spatial dimensions: *height* (up/down), *width* (left/right) and *depth* (forwards/backwards)

Three-gauge bosons (photon, gluon, W&Z bosons)

Three types of elementary particles *(leptons, quarks, gauge bosons)*

Three quarks in every proton *(two "up" and one "down")*

Three primary colors of light *(red, green, blue)*

Three color tone properties *(hue, value, chroma)*

Three laws of motion (*Newton's laws*)

Three laws of planetary motion (*Kepler's laws*)

Three layers of the Sun's interior (*core, radiative zone, convective zone*)

Three layers of the Sun's atmosphere (*photosphere, chromosphere, corona*)

Three types of meteorites (*iron, stony iron, stony*)

Three types of galaxy shapes (*elliptical, spiral, irregular*)

Three substances of the universe (*normal matter, 'dark matter', 'dark energy'*)

Three phases of the moon (*new moon, first quarter, full moon*)

Three planetary regions (*temperate, sub-tropical, tropical*)

Three layers of the Earth (*crust, mantle, core*)

Three components of an ecosystem (*producers, consumers, decomposers*)

Three types of rocks (*igneous, sedimentary, metamorphic*)

Three types of fossil fuels (*coal, crude oil, natural gas*)

Three hydrological processes (*evaporation, condensation, precipitation*)

Three basic types of (meteorological) precipitation (*liquid, freezing, frozen*)

Three types of substances *(mono-constituent, multi-constituent, UVCB)*

Three phases of (normal) matter *(solid, liquid, gas)*

Three types of covalent chemical bonds *(single, double and triple bonds)*

Three isotopes of hydrogen *(protium, deuterium, tritium)*

Three atoms in each molecule of water *(two hydrogen atoms and an oxygen atom)*

Three endings to salts *(-ide, -ite, -ate)*

Three requirements for fire *(fuel, oxygen, heat)*

Three nucleotide bases in a genetic codon

Three domains of life *(archaea, bacteria and eukaryotes)*

Three major groups of flowering plants *(monocots, eudicots, magnolids)*

Three major functions that are basic to plant growth and development: *(photosynthesis* [making sugars], *respiration* [metabolizing those sugars], and *transpiration* [water vapor loss]

Three things that the chlorophyll in plants needs for photosynthesis to take place: *(sunlight, carbon dioxide and water)*

Transpiration serves three roles: *(cooling the plant, moving minerals* and *sugars through the plant,* and *maintaining the turgidity pressure* [stiffness] *of the plant's cells)*

Three parts of an insect's body *(head, thorax, abdomen)*

<u>BIOLOGY</u>

Three types of cones in the retina, relating to the three primary colors

Three semi-circular canals in the ear *(lateral, anterior, posterior)*

Three sections in the ear *(outer, middle, inner)*

Three ossicles in the middle ear *(malleus, incus, stapes)*

Three segments to each limb *(proximal, mid, distal)*

Three bones in each arm *(humerus, radius, ulna)*

Three joints in the arm *(shoulder, elbow, wrist)*

Three joints in the leg *(hip, knee, ankle)*

Three joints in the elbow *(humeroulnar, humeroradial, proximal radioulnar)*

Three functional compartments in the knee joint *(the femoropatellar, medial femorotibial* and *lateral femorotibial articulations)*

Three types of fibrous joints *(sutures, gomphoses, syndesmoses)*

Three types of bone in each hand (*carpals, metacarpals, phalanges*)

Three types of bone in each foot (*tarsals, metatarsals, phalanges*)

Three bones (phalanges) in each finger and in each toe (*proximal, intermediate, distal*)

Three layers of skin (*dermis, epidermis, hypodermis*)

Three components of a cell (*cell membrane, nucleus, cytoplasm*)

Three types of blood vessels (*arteries, veins, capillaries*)

Three types of blood cells [*red* (erythrocytes), *white* (leukocytes), *platelets* (thrombocytes)]

Three processes of the intestinal tract (*ingestion, digestion, excretion*)

Three germ layers (*Endoderm, Mesoderm, Ectoderm*)

Three parts of a human tooth (*crown, neck, root*)

Three organs of otolaryngology (*ear, nose, throat*)

Three major body systems (*digestive, circulatory, respiratory*)

Three parts to a neuron: (*soma* [*cell body*], *axon, dendrites*)

Three main parts of the brain (*forebrain, midbrain, hindbrain*)

Three parts of the forebrain (*cerebrum, thalamus, hypothalamus*)

Three parts of the midbrain (*colliculi, tegmentum, cerebral peduncles*)

Three parts of the hindbrain (*cerebellum, pons, medulla*)

Three membranes enclosing the brain (*dura mater, arachnoid, pia mater*)

The brain operates on three levels: *consciously* (for cognitive thought and declarative memory); *subconsciously* (for pre-planned actions and procedural memory); and *unconsciously* (for breathing, heart beating, etc.)

Our conscious mind is fed from three sources: *our senses* (which can be fooled); *our memory* (which is flawed); and *our imagination* (which is inventive)

Three aspects of the human mind (*memory, intellect, will*)

Three parts of the human personality (*id, ego, superego*)

The sum of human capacity consists of three abilities (*thought, word and deed*)

Three times of man (*birth, life, death*)

Three periods of the Gait Cycle (*initial double limb support, single limb support, and terminal double limb support*)

<u>MUSIC</u>

Three types of musical notes (*sharps, flats, naturals*)

Three aspects of a song (*lyrics, melody, rhythm*)

Three types of musical chords (*root, third, fifth*)

MATHEMATICS

Three types of a real number (*positive, negative, zero*)

Three parts to any arithmetic operation: for addition: *augend, addend and sum* - for subtraction: *minuend, subtrahend and difference* - for multiplication: *multiplicand, multiplier and product* - for division: *dividend, divisor and quotient*

Three laws of arithmetic operations (*commutative, associative, distributive*)

Three types of equivalence relation (*reflexivity, symmetry, transitivity*)

Three types of symmetry operations (*translation, rotation, reflection*)

Three geometries (*Euclidean, spherical, hyperbolic*)

The number 3 is the basis of an entire branch of mathematics, called trigonometry (from the Greek *trigonon* "triangle" + *metron* "measure")

Three trigonometric functions (*sine, cosine, tangent*)

Three types of average (*mean, mode, median*)

GRAMMAR

Three logical operators (*AND, OR and NOT*)

Three laws of logic (*identity, noncontradiction, excluded middle*)

Three parts of a logical syllogism (*major premise, minor premise, conclusion*)

Three grammatical parts to a sentence (*subject, verb, complement*)

Three persons in grammar [*1st person* (I/we), *2nd* (you or your), *3rd* (he/she/it/they)]

Three genders in grammar [*masculine* (he/him), *feminine* (she/her), *neuter* (it)]

Three forms of comparison in grammar [*positive, comparative* (more, -er), *superlative* (most, -est)]

Three cases in (English) grammar [*subjective/nominative* (he), *objective/accusative* (him) and *possessive/genitive* (his)]

Three parts of a narrative (*beginning, middle, end*)

Components of an essay (*introduction, body, conclusion*)

Elements of a rhetorical appeal (*ethos, pathos, logos*)

Aspects of a story (*plot, characters, setting*)

<u>RELIGION</u>

The Creator – *omniscient, omnipotent, omnipresent*

Christian God – *Father, Son, Holy Spirit*

Jesus – *The Way, The Truth, The Life*

Ancient Near East- *Qudshu, Astarte, Anat*

Classical Antiquity – Many dieties came in threes

Hinduism – Para Brahman is *Brahma, Visnu, Shiva*

Ancient Celtic Cultures – *many example of triad dieties*

Buddhism – *The three jewels*

Taoism – *The three pure ones*

Islam – *Fear, Hope and Love*

Baha'i - *Intention, Power and Action*

Confucianism – *Benevolence, Wisdom and Courage*

<u>OTHER TRIUNE EXAMPLES</u>

3 Coins in a Fountain

3 Days of the Condor

3 Miles in a League

3 Goals in a Hat Trick

3 Piece Suit

3 Feet in a Yard

3 Books in Lord of the Rings

3 Ring Circus

3 Ships of Christopher Columbus

3 Sheets to the Wind

3 Books in a Trilogy

3 Wheels on a Tricycle

3 Wise Men

3-Legged Race

3 Ring Circus

3-Wheeler

3 Cornered Hat

3 Dimensional

3 Musketeers

3 R's (reading, 'riting, 'rithmatic)

3 Sides of a triangle

3 Races in the Triple Crown (horse racing)

3 Angles in a Triangle

3 Trimesters in a Pregnancy

3 Flavors in Neapolitan Ice Cream

3 Stars in Orion's belt

3 Barleycorns in an Inch

3 Hands on a Clock (with the Seconds Hand)

3 Colors in a Flag

3 Minute Egg

3 Great Pyramids at Giza

3 Holes in a Bowling Ball

3 Colors in a Set of Traffic Lights

3 Minutes in a Boxing Round

3 Teaspoons in a Tablespoon

3 Legs on a Stool

3 Monastic Vows (Obience, Stability, Conversatio Morum)

3 Body Types: Endomorph, Mesomorph, Ectomorph

3 Ring Notebooks

3 Germ layers: Endoderm, Mesoderm, Ectoderm

3 Species of Homo: Homo habilis, Homo erectus, Homo sapiens

3 Basic parts of a camera: Lens, Shutter, Sensor

3 Stages of a Project lifecycle: initiation, planning, execution

The Truth, The Whole Truth and Nothing but the Truth

Life, Liberty and the Pursuit of Happiness

Hear no Evil, See no Evil, Speak no Evil

National motto of France/Haiti: Liberty, Equality, Fraternity

Paper, Rock, Scissors

Ready, Aim, Fire

On Your mark, Get Set, Go

Olympic medals of gold, silver, bronze

Types of joints (ball & socket, hinge, pivot)

Stages of a rocket launch (launch, orbit, re-entry)

Parts of a joke (setup, delivery, punchline)

Primary components of a transistor (emitter, base, collector)

Primary components of an airplane (fuselage, wings, empennage)

Basic components of a computer: CPU, memory, storage

Three phases in the development of technology (*eotechnic* [*mechanical*], *paleotechnic* [*steam-powered*] and *neotechnic* [*electric-powered*]

Communication systems require three components (*transmitter, channel, receiver*)

The list goes on. See if you can find more examples as they are everywhere in our universe! Now that you know that life works in threes (with proof!), we can begin to apply this concept to whatever topics we want.

So, to overcome struggles with abundance, we need to apply the three areas that abundance consists of – HEALTH, MONEY, PROVISIONS. Let's get started!

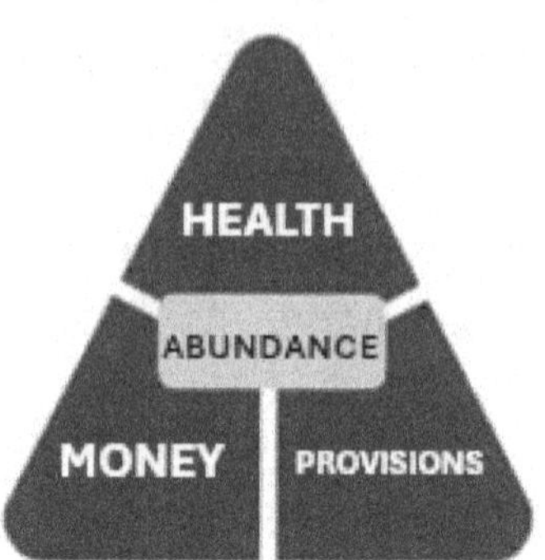

HEALTH
ABUNDANCE
MONEY
PROVISIONS

ABUNDANCE

At times, questions are asked "What is the purpose of life?" or "What is the meaning of life?" But the real question we need to ask is..." What is life about?" The answer is – Life is about going after what you need and want. You can't have what you want until you get what you need. What do we need? We need *good health, money and provisions*...all at the same time preferably.

Having **good health** is like having a superpower that enhances every aspect of our lives. It's not just about feeling physically strong and energetic but also about being able to fully enjoy each day with vitality and enthusiasm. When we're in good health, we can pursue our passions, engage in activities we love, and build meaningful relationships without the hindrance of physical limitations. It allows us to handle life's challenges with resilience and optimism, knowing that we have the strength to bounce back. Good health is truly a gift that empowers us to live our best lives, nurturing our well-being and enabling us to create lasting memories with the people we cherish.

Having **money** can bring a lot of positive changes to our lives. It's not just about being able to afford luxuries or comfort—it's about having the freedom to make choices that align with our dreams and values. Money provides security, allowing us to take care of ourselves and our loved ones, whether it's through good healthcare, quality education, or creating a stable home environment. It also opens doors to new opportunities, whether it's traveling to new places, pursuing hobbies, or investing in personal growth. Moreover, having financial resources can alleviate stress and provide peace of mind, knowing that we have the means to handle unexpected challenges and plan for the future. Ultimately, money, when used wisely, can enhance our quality of life and enable us to contribute positively to the world around us.

Living a decent life is about having access to the essentials that allow us to thrive with dignity and fulfillment. It starts with having a safe and comfortable place to call home, where we feel secure and can relax after a long day. Access to nutritious food and clean water is crucial for our health and well-being, ensuring we have the energy and vitality to pursue our goals. Education plays a vital role in expanding our knowledge and skills, opening up opportunities for personal growth and meaningful employment. Additionally, access to healthcare services ensures that we can maintain our physical and mental well-being, addressing any health issues promptly. Finally, a supportive community and social connections provide emotional nourishment, fostering a sense of belonging and mutual respect. These **provisions** form the foundation of a decent life, enabling us to live with dignity and contribute positively to our communities.

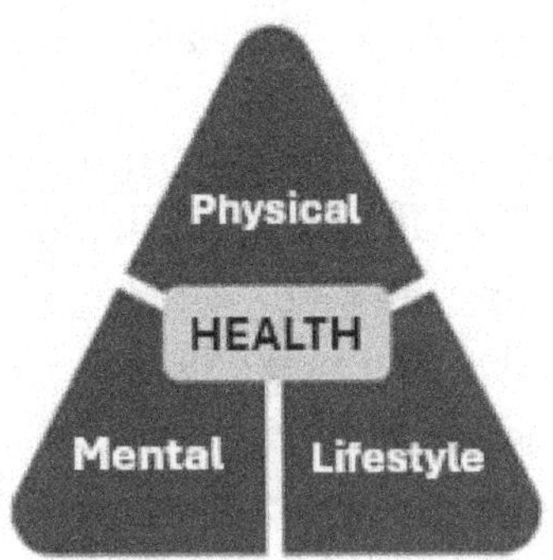
Physical
HEALTH
Mental
Lifestyle

GOOD HEALTH

Good health isn't just about feeling okay; it's about feeling fantastic, inside and out! When we talk about good health, we're looking at a few key things that help us live our best lives. First off, it's all about **physical** well-being. That means keeping our bodies strong and active, whether it's through regular exercise, eating nutritious foods, or getting enough sleep. Taking care of ourselves physically sets the foundation for everything else we do.

But wait, there's more to it than just that! **Mental** and emotional health are also super important. Feeling good in our minds means managing stress, finding ways to relax, and building positive relationships with others. It's about being kind to ourselves and knowing when to ask for help if we need it. When our mental and emotional health are in sync with our physical well-being, we're really firing on all cylinders!

And let's not forget about **lifestyle** choices. Good health often comes from making smart decisions every day. That could mean choosing to quit smoking, limiting alcohol intake, or staying away from harmful substances. It's also about finding a balance that works for us, whether it's work, play, or simply taking time to unwind. Ultimately, good health is about feeling strong, happy, and ready to tackle whatever life throws our way. So let's raise a glass (of water, of course!) to staying healthy and living our best lives!

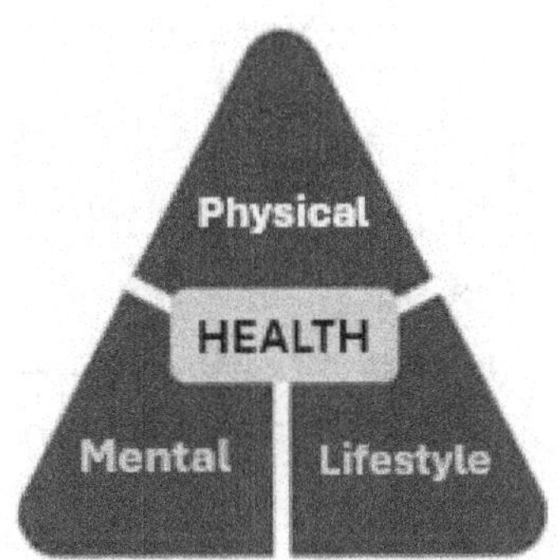
Physical
HEALTH
Mental
Lifestyle

Physical

Achieving a healthy physical well-being is like building a strong foundation for a happy life. It starts with staying active. Regular exercise doesn't have to mean hitting the gym for hours – it could be as simple as taking a daily walk, dancing to your favorite tunes, or playing a sport you enjoy. Moving our bodies keeps our muscles strong, our hearts healthy, and our energy levels up!

Next up, let's talk about nutrition. Eating well isn't about strict diets or counting calories; it's about nourishing our bodies with the good stuff. That means filling our plates with a colorful variety of fruits, vegetables, whole grains, and lean proteins. It's about enjoying food that fuels us and makes us feel good from the inside out. And hey, treating ourselves occasionally is part of a balanced approach – a little chocolate or a slice of pizza can be good for the soul!

Of course, getting enough rest is also crucial. Sleep isn't just for recharging our batteries; it's when our bodies repair and rejuvenate themselves. Aim for those seven to nine hours a night, create a relaxing bedtime routine, and give yourself the gift of quality sleep. When we combine regular activity, nourishing foods, and restful sleep, we're well on our way to achieving a healthy physical well-being that supports a vibrant, active lifestyle. Here's to feeling strong, energized, and ready to take on the world!

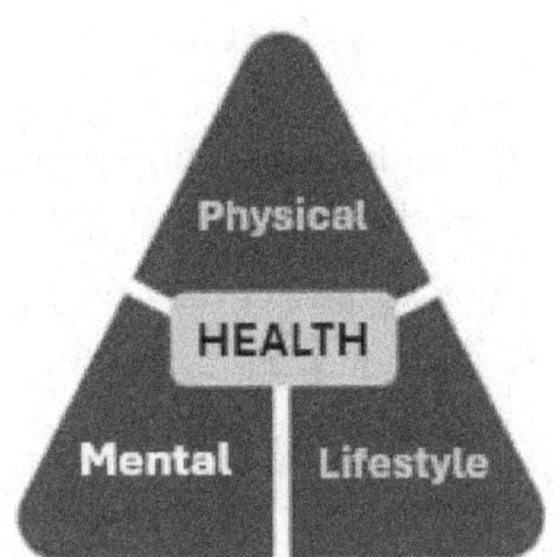
Physical
HEALTH
Mental
Lifestyle

Mental

Taking care of our mental and emotional well-being is just as important as looking after our physical health. It's like giving our minds a big hug! One key aspect is managing stress. Life can throw curveballs but finding ways to cope – whether through deep breathing, meditation, or talking things out with a friend – can really help. It's about finding what works best for you to keep that stress in check and your mind feeling clear and focused.

Another biggie is nurturing positive relationships. Surrounding ourselves with supportive, uplifting people can do wonders for our mental health. Whether it's family, friends, or even furry companions, having that network of love and understanding can make tough times feel a little lighter and the good times even sweeter. And don't forget, being kind to yourself is crucial too. We all have moments when we're our own worst critics, but practicing self-compassion and treating ourselves with the same kindness we give to others can make a world of difference.

Lastly, finding joy in the little things is a big part of maintaining good mental and emotional health. Whether it's indulging in a hobby, spending time in nature, or simply savoring a delicious meal, taking moments to appreciate the beauty and positivity around us can lift our spirits and keep us feeling balanced. When we combine stress management, positive relationships, self-compassion, and a sprinkle of joy, we're nurturing our mental and emotional well-being in a way that helps us thrive and embrace life with open arms. Here's to a happy, healthy mind and heart!

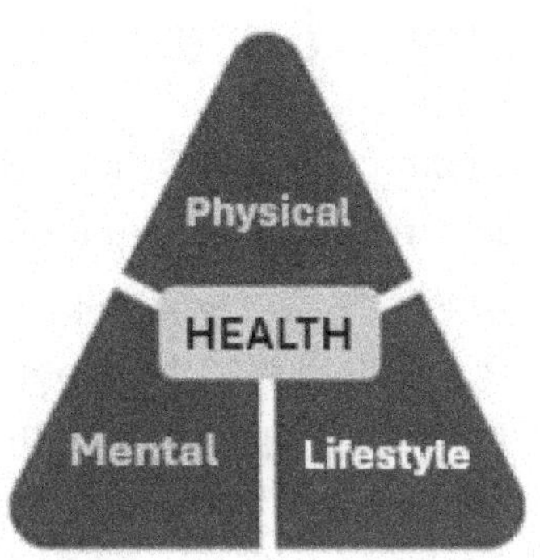

Physical
HEALTH
Mental
Lifestyle

Lifestyle

Making healthy lifestyle choices is like giving ourselves a gift that keeps on giving – it's all about setting ourselves up for a life full of vitality and happiness. When we choose to eat nutritious foods, move our bodies regularly, and prioritize restful sleep, we're investing in our long-term health. These choices not only help us maintain a healthy weight and reduce the risk of chronic illnesses like heart disease and diabetes but also boost our energy levels and mood. It's like giving ourselves a daily dose of sunshine!

On the flip side, making poor lifestyle choices can have consequences that can dampen our spirits. Whether it's smoking, excessive drinking, or indulging in unhealthy foods too often, these habits can negatively impact our physical health, mental well-being, and overall quality of life. They can increase the risk of serious health issues and leave us feeling drained and unmotivated. But fear not! Every day is a new opportunity to make positive changes.

By making healthy lifestyle choices, we're not just taking care of ourselves in the moment; we're also setting a powerful example for those around us. Whether it's our friends, family, or even our pets, our choices ripple out and inspire others to prioritize their health too. It's like spreading a wave of positivity! So let's raise a glass (of water, of course!) to making those smart choices that support our well-being and help us live our best lives. Here's to feeling strong, happy, and ready to conquer whatever comes our way!

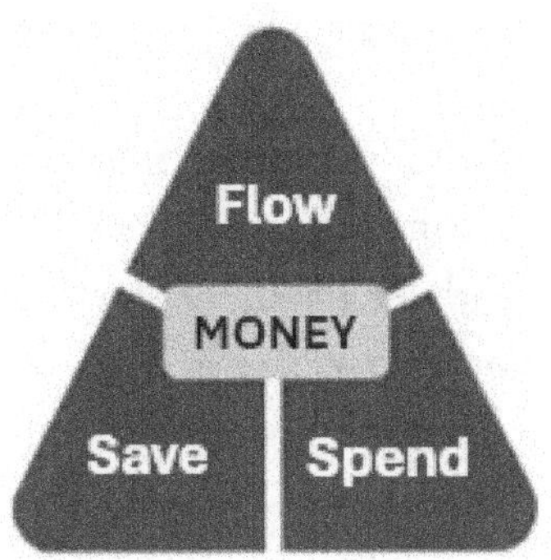

Flow
MONEY
Save
Spend

MONEY

Let's take a fun trip back in time to when the idea of money first popped up in human history. Picture this: way back in ancient times, people started trading goods with each other. Maybe someone had an extra bushel of grain, and another person had a shiny rock they didn't need. They figured out that by swapping these items, they could both get something they wanted. Pretty cool, right?

As communities grew and trading became more common, people started to realize that some items were easier to trade than others. Imagine trying to carry around a herd of sheep just to buy a loaf of bread – not very practical! So, clever folks came up with the idea of using something that everyone agreed had value, like shiny metals or rare shells. These became the first forms of money – objects that represented worth and made trading a whole lot easier.

Fast forward a bit, and civilizations around the world began to create coins made from metals like gold and silver. These were stamped with symbols to show their value and became a universal way to buy and sell goods. Eventually, paper money came into play, making transactions even simpler. Today, we've got digital money flying around the internet! It's amazing how an idea born out of simple trading has evolved into the complex financial systems we use today. So, next time you pull out your wallet or tap your phone to pay, remember you're part of a long, fascinating history of human ingenuity and creativity in making life a little more convenient for everyone!

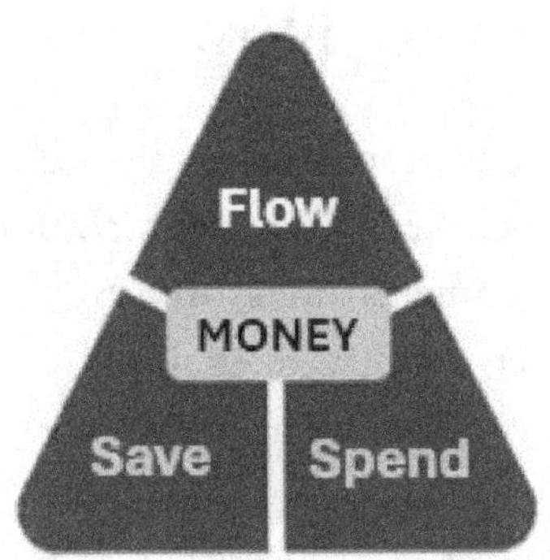
Flow
MONEY
Save
Spend

Flow

When it comes to earning money, there's a wide world of work out there waiting for us to explore. Let's start with traditional jobs. These are the ones you might find in offices, shops, or factories – like being a teacher, a nurse, a chef, or even a software engineer. These jobs often involve working for a company or organization, where you exchange your time and skills for a paycheck. They provide stability and a regular income, which can be reassuring when planning for the future.

Then there's freelance and gig work. This type of work is all about flexibility and independence. Freelancers are their own bosses, offering services like graphic design, writing, tutoring, or driving for ride-sharing apps. Gig work often involves short-term projects or tasks, like delivering groceries or renting out a spare room through platforms like Airbnb. It's a great way to earn money on your own schedule and explore different interests and skills.

And let's not forget about entrepreneurship! Starting your own business is like planting a seed and watching it grow into something amazing. Whether it's opening a bakery, launching a tech startup, or selling handmade crafts online, entrepreneurship is all about taking risks, being creative, and turning your passion into profit. It can be challenging, but also incredibly rewarding, as you have the freedom to shape your own destiny and create something that brings value to others.

So whether you're drawn to a traditional job with stability, the freedom of freelance work, or the excitement of entrepreneurship, there's a world of opportunities out there to earn money doing what you love. Finding the right path for you might take some exploration and experimentation, but with determination and a positive attitude, you can carve out a fulfilling career that not only pays the bills but also brings you joy and fulfillment. Here's to finding your passion and turning it into a paycheck!

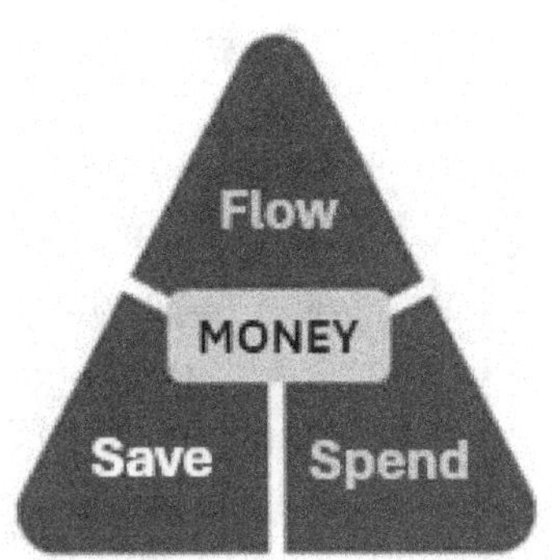
Flow
MONEY
Save
Spend

Save

Paying yourself first isn't just about finances—it's a philosophy that can transform how you approach your goals and wellbeing. Imagine your paycheck as a fresh batch of cookies straight out of the oven. Before you start handing them out to everyone else (bills, groceries, that cute new outfit you spotted), you take a moment to set aside a few for yourself. It's not selfish; it's smart. By putting aside, a portion of your income right off the bat—whether it's for savings, investments, or your rainy-day fund—you're ensuring that your future needs are covered.

Think of it like tending to your own garden before watering your neighbor's plants. When you prioritize yourself financially, you're setting the stage for greater peace of mind and security down the road. It's like giving a little gift to your future self—a gesture that says, "I've got your back." Whether you're squirreling away for that dream vacation, building an emergency fund, or investing in your long-term goals, paying yourself first is a powerful habit that builds financial resilience and confidence.

Moreover, paying yourself first isn't just about money; it's a mindset that can spill over into other areas of your life. It teaches you the value of self-care and the importance of nurturing your own dreams alongside your responsibilities. By making this a habit, you're cultivating a sense of empowerment and control over your financial destiny. It's about taking charge and saying, "I deserve to build a better future for myself." So, next time you're divvying up that paycheck, remember to set aside a slice for you—it's not just about what you're saving, but what you're investing in: your own happiness and peace of mind.

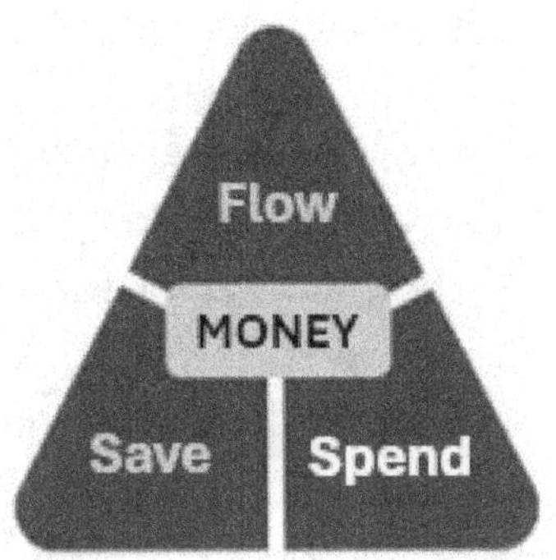

Flow
MONEY
Save
Spend

Spend Wisely

Spending wisely is like navigating through a buffet—there are so many tempting options, but you know that loading up on everything might not leave you feeling your best afterward. It's about making choices that align with your priorities and long-term goals. When you spend wisely, you're not just stretching your dollars; you're investing in what truly matters to you. Whether it's saving up for that dream vacation, building a nest egg, or supporting causes close to your heart, every dollar spent thoughtfully is a step toward financial freedom and peace of mind.

Think of it as building a sturdy house—one where each brick is carefully chosen to withstand the test of time. When you make intentional spending decisions, you're laying a foundation for a more secure future. It's not about depriving yourself of joy but finding ways to maximize the value you get from every dollar. Whether you're comparing prices, hunting for deals, or simply pausing to ask yourself, "Do I really need this?" you're cultivating a habit that pays off in more ways than one.

Moreover, spending wisely isn't just about the numbers; it's about fostering a mindset of gratitude and contentment. It's recognizing the difference between fleeting impulses and lasting satisfaction. By making conscious choices about where your money goes, you're not only shaping your financial landscape but also cultivating a sense of empowerment and control over your life. So, next time you reach for your wallet, remember that each purchase is an opportunity to invest in your future—choose wisely, and watch your dreams take shape.

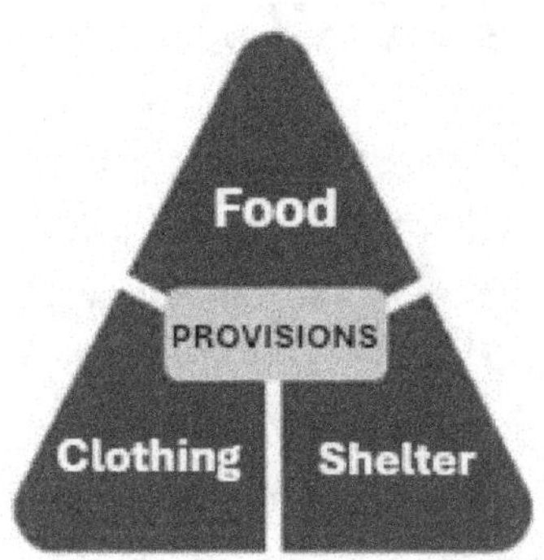

Food
PROVISIONS
Clothing
Shelter

PROVISIONS

Remember that provisions are something that we need before we can go after what we want. Having the essentials of food, clothing, and shelter forms the sturdy foundation of a sustainable and fulfilling life. Let's start with food – it's not just about satisfying hunger; it's about nourishing our bodies with the nutrients they need to thrive. Whether it's enjoying a home-cooked meal with loved ones or savoring fresh produce from a local market, **food** connects us to our communities and cultures. It's like fuel for our bodies and souls, keeping us energized and ready to tackle each day with gusto.

Clothing goes beyond fashion; it's about protection and self-expression. From cozy sweaters in winter to breathable fabrics in summer, clothing shields us from the elements while allowing us to express our personal style. It's like wearing confidence on our sleeves! When we have access to clothing that meets our needs and reflects our identity, it enhances our well-being and strengthens our sense of self.

And then there's **shelter** – our safe haven from the world. Whether it's a cozy apartment, a suburban house, or a rural retreat, having a place to call home provides stability and security. It's where we rest, recharge, and create memories with family and friends. Shelter isn't just about four walls and a roof; it's about belonging and feeling grounded in our environment. When we have a safe and comfortable place to live, it allows us to focus on pursuing our dreams and contributing positively to our communities.

In essence, having provisions of food, clothing, and shelter isn't just about meeting basic needs; it's about cultivating a sustainable and meaningful life. It's about embracing gratitude for the essentials that support our well-being and enable us to live fully. So, here's to cherishing the simple joys of a good meal, feeling comfortable in our own skin, and finding solace in the place we call home. Here's to living sustainably and appreciating the blessings that enrich our lives every day!

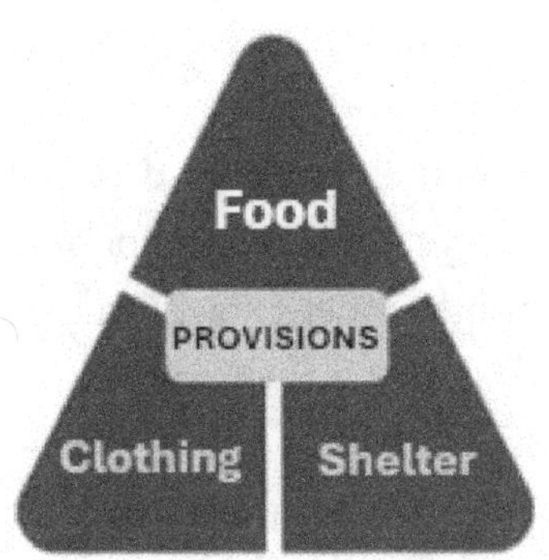

Food
PROVISIONS
Clothing
Shelter

Food

Eating balanced meals that include good carbohydrates, protein, and healthy fats is like giving your body a symphony of nutrients that keep it humming along smoothly. Let's start with carbohydrates – they're your body's preferred source of energy, like fuel for a car. **Good carbohydrates**, found in foods like whole grains, fruits, and vegetables, provide a steady release of energy throughout the day. They help keep you feeling satisfied and ready to take on whatever comes your way, whether it's a busy workday or a fun-filled weekend.

Next up, **protein** is like the building blocks for your body. It's essential for repairing tissues, supporting immune function, and building strong muscles. Good sources of protein include lean meats, fish, eggs, beans, nuts, and tofu. Including protein in your meals helps maintain muscle mass, supports a healthy metabolism, and keeps you feeling fuller longer. It's like giving your body the tools it needs to stay strong and resilient.

And let's not forget about **good fats** – they're not just tasty; they're crucial for overall health. Healthy fats, found in foods like avocados, nuts, seeds, and olive oil, provide essential fatty acids that support brain function, hormone production, and heart health. They're like the lubrication that keeps your body's engine running smoothly. Including good fats in your diet helps maintain healthy cholesterol levels and promotes a feeling of satisfaction after meals.

Eating balanced meals that include good carbohydrates, protein, and healthy fats is key to supporting your overall health and well-being. It's not about strict diets or deprivation; it's about enjoying a variety of nutritious foods that nourish your body and provide the energy you need to live your best life. By making mindful choices and incorporating these essential nutrients into your meals, you're setting yourself up for long-term health and vitality. Here's to savoring delicious, balanced meals that fuel your body and nourish your soul!

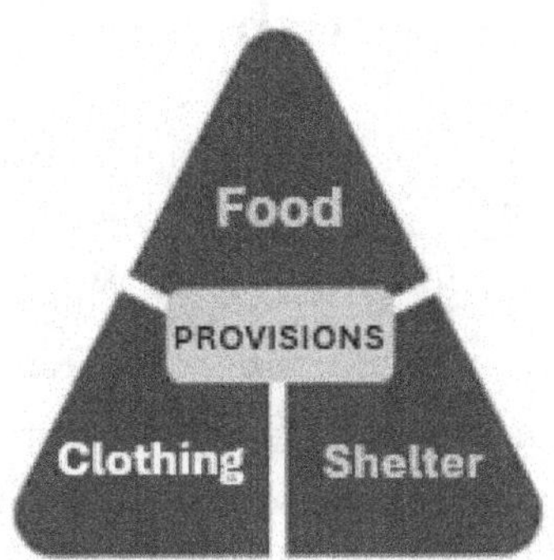
Food
PROVISIONS
Clothing
Shelter

Clothing

When it comes to clothing, there's a balance between meeting our basic needs and indulging in fashion trends. Let's start with the basics – having clothing that suits our daily activities and climate is essential. It's like having a reliable toolkit for life. From sturdy jeans and cozy sweaters in colder months to breathable fabrics and comfortable shoes in warmer weather, these basics provide practicality and comfort. They protect us from the elements and help us feel confident and ready to take on the day.

However, the allure of fashion trends can be irresistible. It's like adding a splash of excitement and personality to our wardrobe. Following trends can be fun and creative, allowing us to express ourselves and stay current with what's happening in the world of style. Yet, it's important to approach fashion trends mindfully. Investing in timeless pieces and versatile staples ensures that our wardrobe remains functional and adaptable over time. It's like building a wardrobe that stands the test of time, where each piece serves a purpose and can be mixed and matched effortlessly.

Ultimately, finding a balance between basic necessities and fashion trends is about making thoughtful choices that align with our lifestyle and values. It's about prioritizing quality, sustainability, and personal style while avoiding unnecessary spending on fleeting trends. By investing in well-made essentials and incorporating trends mindfully, we can cultivate a wardrobe that not only meets our practical needs but also reflects our individuality and evolves with us over time. Here's to dressing with intention, enjoying the creativity of fashion, and embracing a style that speaks authentically to who we are!

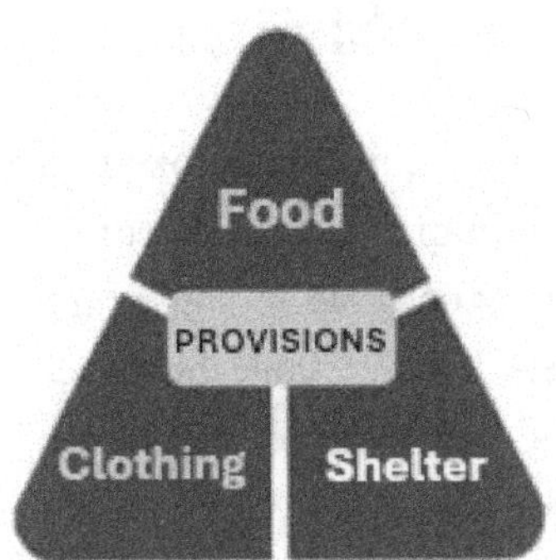

Food
PROVISIONS
Clothing
Shelter

Shelter

Having a stable home is like having a cozy nest where everyone in the family can feel safe, supported, and nurtured. It provides a sense of security and belonging, which are fundamental for emotional well-being. When family members have a stable home environment, it creates a foundation where they can thrive and grow. Whether it's a small apartment or a spacious house, having a place to call home fosters a sense of stability that enhances overall happiness and strengthens family bonds.

Moreover, a stable home promotes routine and structure, which are crucial for maintaining a healthy lifestyle. It's like having a reliable anchor in the midst of life's ups and downs. From bedtime routines to family meals and shared activities, a stable home provides predictability and a sense of continuity. This consistency supports children's development, helps adults manage stress, and encourages open communication within the family. It's a place where memories are made, traditions are cherished, and everyone can feel grounded and connected.

Lastly, a stable home serves as a sanctuary where family members can recharge and rejuvenate. It's like a retreat from the outside world, where individuals can unwind, relax, and find solace after a busy day. Having a comfortable and peaceful environment promotes physical health and mental well-being. It's a place where laughter echoes through the halls, dreams are nurtured, and love is cultivated. By prioritizing stability in our homes, we create a nurturing space where all family members can flourish and thrive together. Here's to the warmth and joy of a stable home that enriches our lives and strengthens our bonds every day!

SUMMARY

Chasing after riches, mind-altering substances, or accumulating possessions can sometimes lead us down a path that doesn't necessarily bring lasting happiness or fulfillment. Let's start with the pursuit of riches. While financial success and security are important, placing too much emphasis on wealth can overshadow other aspects of life that contribute to well-being. It's like chasing a mirage that promises fulfillment but often leaves us feeling empty. True wealth is found in experiences, relationships, and personal growth – things that money alone can't buy.

Similarly, turning to mind-altering substances as a means of escape or pleasure can have serious consequences. It's like trying to fill a void temporarily without addressing underlying issues or emotions. Substance use can affect our health, relationships, and overall quality of life. Seeking happiness through substances is like chasing a fleeting high that ultimately fades, leaving us craving more and potentially harming ourselves and those around us in the process.

Lastly, accumulating possessions beyond our genuine needs can clutter our lives and distract us from what truly matters. It's like filling a room with things we think will bring us happiness, only to realize they don't fulfill us in the way we hoped. Material possessions can weigh us down mentally and financially, creating stress and complicating our lives. True contentment comes from appreciating what we have, cultivating meaningful connections, and finding joy in experiences rather than things.

In conclusion, while it's natural to seek comfort, security, and pleasure in life, it's important to do so in ways that promote genuine well-being and long-term happiness. By focusing on relationships, personal growth, and living with intention, we can cultivate a fulfilling life that goes beyond superficial pursuits. Let's prioritize what truly matters and embrace a journey that brings us lasting happiness and fulfillment.

Invitation

There is an expression that "Less is more." The less stuff you have in your life...the more freedom you will have from worry. If you don't need much, then you're not held prisoner by having to always accumulate things. I think it really comes down to appetite. If you have a small appetite for possessions, then that's okay. If your appetite is moderate, more power to you. Should your appetite be huge, then maybe spending your life accumulating things is the way to go.

Sometimes possessions can be like a mirage where we rush to get there but eventually long for something else. Nothing seems to ever satiate our desires. Always looking for the next best thing or deal. There's a term for this known as: **SOS** - Shiny Object Syndrome.

My invitation is to try each path and see what works for you. You never know till you try and at the end of your life it's always preferable to have no regrets. When my mother was breathing her last breath, I stood at her bedside, and she said to me "I wish I had gone to New Zealand. I had the money but kept putting it off, thinking I would go there the following year."

We have the whole world and universe in front of us...how much do you want to bite off during your lifetime?

When you're with someone who is sharing their struggles with you...just smile at him/her and give them one of these. He/she will ask "What is that?" Then simply reply "Life Works in Threes."

Other titles coming out:

- Weight Struggles?
- Life Struggles?
- Parenting Struggles?
- Romance Struggles?
- Purpose Struggles?
- Happiness Struggles?
- Sales Struggles?
- Speaker Struggles?
- Time Struggles?
- Network Struggles?
- Marriage Struggles?
- Divorce Struggles?
- Money Struggles?
- Career Struggles?
- Dating Struggles?
- Caretaker Struggles?
- Forgiveness Struggles?
- Grieving Struggles?
- Success Struggles?
- Golf Struggles?
- Workplace Struggles?
- Stress Struggles?
- Shame/Guilt Struggles?
- Addiction Struggles?

Quotes about Abundance

"Abundance is not something we acquire. It is something we tune into." - Wayne Dyer

"When you are grateful, fear disappears, and abundance appears." - Tony Robbins

"There is enough for everyone. If you believe it, if you can see it, if you act from it, it will show up for you. That's the truth." - Michael Beckwith

"Abundance is not about how much you have, it's how you feel about what you have." - Unknown

"The more you have, the more you are occupied. The less you have, the freer you are." - Mother Teresa

Here's a list of various ways you can make money:

1. **Employment**: Get a job with a company or organization where you exchange your time and skills for a salary or wages.
2. **Freelancing**: Offer your skills or services on a freelance basis, such as writing, graphic design, programming, consulting, etc.
3. **Entrepreneurship**: Start your own business or venture, which could involve creating and selling products, offering services, or developing apps and software.
4. **Investing**: Invest in stocks, bonds, real estate, or other assets that have the potential to generate income or appreciate in value.
5. **Side hustles**: Take on part-time or gig work outside of your regular job, such as driving for rideshare services, delivering food, or selling handmade crafts.
6. **Online platforms**: Make money through online platforms like YouTube (ad revenue and sponsorships), Twitch (subscriptions and donations), Etsy (selling handmade goods), and others.
7. **Renting or leasing**: Rent out property you own, such as a room in your house, a vacation home, or equipment like cameras or tools.
8. **Teaching and tutoring**: Offer your knowledge and expertise by teaching classes, tutoring students, or creating online courses.
9. **Monetizing hobbies**: Turn your hobbies or passions into income sources, such as photography, gaming, baking, or fitness coaching.
10. **Passive income**: Generate income that requires

minimal effort to maintain, such as dividends from stocks, royalties from books or music, or affiliate marketing.

11. **Consulting**: Provide specialized advice and services to businesses or individuals based on your expertise in a particular field.

12. **Content creation**: Create and monetize content through blogging, podcasting, writing ebooks, or creating and selling digital products.

13. **Event planning**: Organize and host events, conferences, or workshops for which you charge admission or receive sponsorships.

14. **Peer-to-peer lending**: Lend money to individuals or businesses through peer-to-peer lending platforms in exchange for interest payments.

15. **Flipping items**: Buy and resell items for a profit, either online (e.g., eBay, Craigslist) or through local markets and flea markets.

These are just a few ideas to get you started, and the feasibility of each option can depend on factors such as your skills, resources, and interests.

Here's a list of various ways you can invest money:

1. **Stocks**: Buy shares of ownership in a company, with the potential to earn returns through dividends and capital appreciation.
2. **Bonds**: Invest in debt securities issued by governments or corporations, which pay periodic interest and return the principal amount at maturity.
3. **Mutual Funds**: Pool your money with other investors to invest in a diversified portfolio of stocks, bonds, or other securities managed by a professional fund manager.
4. **Exchange-Traded Funds (ETFs)**: Similar to mutual funds but traded on stock exchanges like individual stocks, offering diversification and often lower fees.
5. **Real Estate**: Invest in residential or commercial properties to generate rental income and potentially benefit from property appreciation.
6. **Real Estate Investment Trusts (REITs)**: Invest in companies that own and operate income-producing real estate properties, which distribute rental income to shareholders.
7. **Certificates of Deposit (CDs)**: Deposit money with a bank for a fixed period at a fixed interest rate, generally offering a higher interest rate than regular savings accounts.
8. **Commodities**: Invest in physical goods like gold, silver, oil, agricultural products, etc., either directly or through commodity futures contracts.
9. **Cryptocurrencies**: Buy and hold digital currencies like Bitcoin, Ethereum, or other cryptocurrencies, which can be highly volatile but offer potential for

high returns.

10. **Annuities**: Purchase insurance products that provide regular payments over a specified period or for life, offering a combination of investment growth and income guarantees.

11. **Peer-to-Peer Lending**: Invest money by lending it to individuals or small businesses through online platforms, earning interest on the loans.

12. **Collectibles**: Invest in items like art, antiques, rare coins, or other collectibles that have the potential to appreciate in value over time.

13. **401(k) or Retirement Accounts**: Contribute to employer-sponsored retirement accounts or individual retirement accounts (IRAs), which offer tax advantages and various investment options.

14. **Hedge Funds and Private Equity**: Invest in professionally managed funds that employ more complex strategies and may have higher minimum investment requirements.

15. **Savings Accounts and Money Market Accounts**: While not traditional investments, these accounts offer safety and liquidity with modest interest earnings.

Each investment option has its own risk profile, potential returns, liquidity, and tax implications, so it's important to consider your financial goals, risk tolerance, and time horizon when choosing how to invest your money.

"Who is richer?

He who has everything or he who needs nothing?"

Remember,

When you get right down to it,

Life is about making choices.

Every day, all day long, that's what we do.

- *We choose to get out of bed or not.*
- *We choose to clean up or not.*
- *We choose what to eat all day.*
- *We choose to exercise or not.*
- *We choose to go to work or not.*
- *We choose to do a good job or not.*
- *We choose to come home or not.*
- *We choose to watch TV or do something constructive.*
- *We choose to bed at a decent hour or not.*

And the next day...we start all over again.

What is the meaning of this? Get good at choosing.

Before you can get good at choosing though...you need to understand how life works in threes.

When someone is struggling with a particular area or two, chances are they are "out of balance" with how life works. How does life work? Life works in threes.

If you're interested in personal topics like life, health, money or business topics like sales, time management and public speaking...TRYUNE WORKS! can shed some light on creating success in those areas.

The definition of TRIUNE is a group of three things; united. Being three in one, such as - humans are *mental, physical* and *spiritual beings.* The word TRYUNE is a play of the word TRIUNE, encouraging all to try this concept and help eliminate struggling unnecessarily.

LifeWorksInThrees.com